Wake Up, Oliver!

Wake Up, Oliver!

Leigh Hambly - Kirsten Phillips
Illustrations by María Jesús Álvarez

d books
doubledutch books

"Okay, Teddy. Time to wake up Oliver.
We don't want him to be late for school."

"What a funny dog you are, Teddy."

"I think a belly rub is your favourite thing in the whole wide world."

"What a funny dog you are, Teddy. I think tugging on blankets when I'm making my bed is your favourite thing in the whole wide world. Come on. Time for my shower."

"What a funny dog you are, Teddy. I think washing your face is your favourite thing in the whole wide world."

"What a funny dog you are, Teddy. I think begging for my school lunch is your favourite thing in the whole wide world."

"What a funny dog you are, Teddy. I think my breakfast is your favourite thing in the whole wide world."

"What a funny dog you are, Teddy. I think
a dog chew is your favourite thing
in the whole wide world."

"Harriet will be here soon to walk with me to school. Do you want to play catch while we wait for her?"

"What a funny dog you are, Teddy. I think playing catch is your favourite thing in the whole wide world."

"Look, Harriet is here. After school, we will go for a walk with Harriet and her puppy, Nigel."

"What a funny dog you are, Teddy.
I think giving kisses is your favourite thing
in the whole wide world."

"Teddy is a funny dog, Harriet. Look at him wagging his tail. I think looking out the window is his favourite thing to do!"

"Teddy is a happy dog," Harriet says.

"That's my favourite thing about him in the whole wide world," Oliver says.

Can you find 5 differences in the pictures?

About Teddy

Theodore Bear "Teddy" is an energetic and playful 12-year-old Chihuahua Papillion cross. Teddy is very smart and knows many tricks, which he willingly performs for yummy treats. Many of his favourite things to do are sleeping on his pet parents' pillows, hiding treats, stealing socks, and riding in cars. Some of his least favourite things are getting his nails clipped, puddles, and fireworks. What is Teddy's most favourite thing in the whole wide world? He loves playing at his pet parents' cottage!

High-frequency words*

a	don't	in	soon	when
after	for	is	the	while
and	go	look	to	will
are	her	me	up	with
at	here	my	walk	you
be	him	on	want	your
come	his	out	we	
do	I	play	what	

Other words you need to know

about	dog chew	late	shower	wait
bed	face	lunch	tail	wake
begging	favourite	looking	that's	washing
belly rub	funny	making	thing	whole
blankets	giving	okay	think	wide
breakfast	happy	playing	time	window
catch	I'm	puppy	tugging	world
dog	kisses	school	wagging	

*Referenced from Dolch Word List

Printed in Canada by Friesens

Library and Archives Canada Cataloguing in Publication

Hambly, Leigh, 1952-, author
Wake Up, Oliver! / Leigh Hambly and Kirsten Phillips ; María Jesús Álvarez, illustrator.

(Our neighbourhood)
ISBN 978-0-9940570-1-3 (pbk.)

I. Phillips, Kirsten, 1966-, author II. Álvarez, María Jesús (Illustrator), illustrator III. Title.

PS8615.A412W35 2015 jC813'.6 C2015-902378-5

Doubledutch Books
1427 Somerville Avenue, Winnipeg, Manitoba, R3T 1C3